CAPRICORN

HOROSCOPE

& ASTROLOGY

2020

Capricorn
Horoscope & Astrology
2020

Published by Mystic Shores publications

Suite SM-2380-6403

14601 North Bybee Lake Court

Portland, Oregon 97203

Phone: +1 (805) 308-6503

islandauthor@hotmail.com

Acknowledgment:

Thank you to the stargazers, dreamers, and mystics.
You make this world a better place.

CAPRICORN 2020 OVERVIEW

2020 is an incredible year for Capricorn. Inspiration fans the flames which burn brightly for Capricorn, encouraging new ideas and concepts which inspire growth. Not one, not two, not three, but four Supermoons in 2020 ensures plenty of fantastic energy arrives to inspire Capricorn to develop innovative dreams in tune with their wildest ideas and aspirations. There is astonishing progress to be made towards by following your heart in 2020, Capricorn utilizes the power of Earth to make progress on their most secure goals.

Mercury Retrograde is the most significant destabilizing force in 2020. Forewarned is forearmed and Capricorn does find that bridges can be burnt if not handled sensitively. Being careful with interpersonal relationships allows Capricorn to navigate a delicate path through these troublesome cosmic storms. Capricorn can harness the firepower of their spirit to find solutions and take an affirmative action before relationships veer off course.

2020 is a year which blends the elemental forces of Earth, Air, Fire, and Water with new world technology. This dramatically expands your star signs creative abilities. The star sign Capricorn is one of Earth dominance, and when harnessed correctly, you make remarkable progress as they light the path forward with their burning desires. Inspiration for improving your circumstances with grounded and viable ventures abound for Capricorn in this most incredible year of potentiality.

With so many compelling reasons to shine, the star sign Capricorn can look forward to incredible cosmic energy, which helps increase and boost their potential possible in 2020, and beyond.

Capricorn

Capricorn Dates: December 22 to January 19
Symbol: Goat
Element: Earth
Planet: Saturn
House: Tenth
Colors: Brown, Grey

JANUARY ASTROLOGY

January 3 – First Quarter Moon in Aries.

This Moon phase occurs at 04.45 UTC.

January 3, 4 - Quadrantids Meteor Shower.

The Quadrantids meteor shower run yearly from January 1-5. The Quadrantids meteor shower peaks this year on the night of the 3rd and morning of the 4th.

January 10 - Full Moon in Cancer.

This full moon phase occurs at 19:21 UTC. This full moon is called the Full Wolf Moon because this was the time of year when hungry wolf packs howled outside camps. This full moon has also been known as the Old Moon and the Moon After Yule.

January 10 - Penumbral Lunar Eclipse.

A penumbral lunar eclipse occurs as the Moon passes through the Earth's partial shadow or penumbra. During this type of eclipse, the Moon will darken slightly but won't wholly eclipse. This penumbral eclipse is visible throughout most of Europe, Africa, Asia, and Western Australia.

January 17 – Last Quarter Moon in Libra.

This Moon phase occurs at 12.58 UTC.

January 24 – New Moon in Capricorn.

This new moon phase occurs at 21:42 UTC. The Moon is on the same side of the Earth as the Sun and will not be visible in the night sky. This phase occurs at 21:03 UTC. This is an excellent time to view galaxies and stars as there is no moonlight to obscure your view of the universe.

JANUARY HOROSCOPE

JANUARY WEEK ONE

You breeze into a lively chapter which places a strong emphasis on the sharing of open communication. It does allow you to hit a key milestone in your personal life. You navigate an enterprising time ahead, which places a spotlight on developing long term goals and delight in sharing your thoughts and ideas with another. It could lead to starting a significant assignment, as a passion project soon takes flight. You are rewarded with an enticing path which reconnects you to the wisdom of the ages. It does lead to healing certain aspects which have limited progress, it also rules are a highly imaginative and creative journey, which leads to an expansive vision is taking shape. Mingling with a diverse group sparks exciting meetings of the minds, it does lead to a quest to do purposeful work which benefits others. You reach a turning point, which creates a powerful influence that can help you manifest home based goals. It sets a ball in motion, which could lead to a dream becoming a reality. This begins a bustling time, which kicks off enterprising activities, setting your intention helps you obtain significant progress. Key goals take shape, which corresponds to the advancement of your situation. It does also inspire you to focus on interpersonal relations.

JANUARY WEEK TWO

You think a great deal about past events, it has grown strong values within your spirit. This helps you rise above the drama and focus on your long term goals. You have an unusual ability which is set to be developed further. Even more, clarity arrives in your world soon, and this enhances your ability to spot a little worn avenue, which provides you with an opportunity for growth. If you have a felt restless or unfocused recently, you are going to bring the magic back into your world, it leads to a vibrant chapter where you can enjoy a new zest in your life. As your spirit lifts from the shadows and into the light, you emerge into a more energetic and optimistic chapter, this brings an expansive transit which shapes your trajectory towards growth. It does lead to a goal orientated time, which feels tailor-made for you. It enables you to set your sights on achieving a fantastic outcome. Connecting with an individual who captures your interest does leave you feeling inspired and ready to take on the world. You weed out the time wasters and the ones who drain your energy. It helps you prioritize on achieving a stellar result. This sees things moving forward. You may feel like sorting out areas of your life and tying up loose ends. It creates space to clear the decks so you can begin a new area soon. It is a time where you can reflect on the past and gain insight into your journey so far. Change is tempting you forward, it does shift you towards the development of goals which can provide you with more security.

JANUARY WEEK THREE

You enter a phase which is big and bold, the sun sails into your life with offers of expansion and adventure. It does enable you to make plans to achieve your more significant dreams. Launching into an active phase, you see tangible results flourish. It is a time where you're hungry for new goals and experiences, you seek to connect with others who can add their own thoughts and ideas to this brew of lively potential. You enter a thought-provoking and inspirational chapter which enables you to team up with other adventurers and embark on a fun and exciting time. It leads to impromptu gatherings, it is the perfect time to surround yourself with positive people who understand your need to socialize. It does influence your mind in vibrant ways, and this sparks a bold path which could transform a significant part of your identity. This is a time where you can develop new skills and acquire mastery of a talent. It does reward you with impressive results, and this produces an offer to progress further in your chosen field. Advancement is calling, this tempts you to strengthen your abilities and harness the power of your gifts to further improve your goals. The success which flows into your life eases any pressure you may have been under recently. Nurturing your goals becomes an important focus, you get in touch with the best way to advance your situation. Obstacles are merely an invitation to try an alternative route, you soon discover a path which offers you full steam ahead. A project which has been idling along begins to take off.

JANUARY WEEK FOUR

You discover something on offer, which ties into a long-term goal of yours. At first, details are sparse, but as you streamline and organize in this direction, you discover a new chapter can be launched. You finally can share your talents with a broader audience. A shift forward occurs for you soon, which kicks off an exciting episode. This puts you in a vibrant and energetic phase and connects you with others who hold a similar mindset. It does lead to a charming and transformational time, expanding your horizons provides you with more opportunities to mingle with others and enjoy a highly social aspect. A celebration arrives soon, which brings sincere gratitude into your life. This is a time where you can focus on bringing balance back into your most treasured bonds. There is a search for abundance, which leads to a more grounded and happy chapter. You nurture a situation which helps build a rock-solid environment. Looking ahead with optimism, you soon usher in lighter and brighter days with the ones you care most about. Whatever comes or goes, take this movement to feel sincere gratitude for the bonds you care about.

FEBRUARY ASTROLOGY

February 2 – First Quarter Moon in Taurus. This Moon phase occurs at 1.42 UTC.

February 9 - Full Moon in Leo, Supermoon.

The Moon is on the opposite side of the Earth as the Sun and will be fully illuminated. This phase occurs at 7:33 UTC. This full moon is known as the Full Snow Moon because the heaviest snows usually fall during this month. Since hunting is difficult, this full moon has also been recognized as the Full Hunger Moon, since the harsh weather made fishing difficult. This is the first of four supermoons for 2020. The Moon will be at its nearest approach to the Earth and will look slightly larger and brighter than usual.

February 10 - Mercury at largest Eastern Elongation.

The planet Mercury reaches an eastern elongation of 18.1 degrees from the Sun.

February 15 – Last Quarter Moon in Scorpio.

This Moon phase occurs at 22.17 UTC.

February 18 – Mercury Retrograde begins in Pisces.

During a retrograde period, it isn't the right time to move forward in any practical venture. Be prepared for misunderstandings and miscommunications to be prevalent.

February 23 - New Moon in Aquarius.

The Moon is on the same side of the Earth as the Sun and will not be visible in the night sky. This phase occurs at 15:32 UTC. This is an excellent time to view galaxies and stars as there is no moonlight to obscure your view of the universe.

FEBRUARY HOROSCOPE

FEBRUARY WEEK ONE

The past has afforded you a great deal of wisdom, you are in a quiet phase, which is to do with psychologically processing an intense chapter from a previous situation. Doing this profoundly emotional work has been quite a transformation for you, but you've shed layers, and released areas which no longer serve a purpose in your world. It does create space to emerge and embrace a new chapter of potential. You may be drawn to metaphysical topics soon, it is a restless time which has you feeling thirsty for new horizons. Doing soul-searching, you begin a phase which is more spiritually minded and focused on self-improvement. You also discover new friendships with bohemian types during this chapter, it is a time of exploring and experimenting with new paths. This week speaks of opportunities to improve your life arriving, it brings refreshing dynamics which shine a light on an energizing chapter. This underscores your ability to navigate a course which draws abundance into your world. It does see you being immersed in areas which capture your inspiration, it gives you exciting options to explore, and may even lead to a leap of faith. You can contribute your gifts to a broader audience, it is a time where creativity rules your imagination, you escape into a vision which has you dreaming big about the possibilities. The pace ahead is exciting, you push past barriers and expand your horizons by trying out new adventures. It does lead to more confidence and brings an offer to your table for you to contemplate.

FEBRUARY WEEK TWO

The February 9th Supermoon flows a river of heightened potential into your sphere. You open the floodgates to new potential, the possibilities are endless, but a viable option does stand out which offers you a pertinent path to progress your goals. You barrel forward towards a chapter which enables you to focus on advancement and growth. Unleashing your skills in this area does see a quick succession of positive results. It gives you a yield which is exciting and provides you with further opportunities for growth. There is improvement coming for your family life. It does lead to a more stable environment, and this helps you gain traction on your longer-term goals. A fortuitous streak arrives, which suggests excellent timing, it helps you put together a plan which offers room for growth. Your efforts reap beautiful outcomes, and this builds a sturdy foundation from which to grow your dreams. You are ready to fling the doors open to a fresh start. This heads your energy forward, it activates new potential, and does help you turn over a clean page in your life. It could set you on a bold new beginning, which brings an unexpected path to your door. Initiating essential changes, you create an enjoyable positive shift towards achieving your goals. Exciting outcomes are the result of your willingness to put yourself in new environments. It does bring a change which allows for a transformational change. In hindsight, you will be grateful that you were willing to expand your horizons. It does take you towards a chapter where you craft a bold identity, it positions you better and enables you to make the most of an exciting chapter ahead.

FEBRUARY WEEK THREE

This week sees a flamboyant chapter arriving which features a more social aspect, you discover a tribe of individuals who are lively characters. It does bring you to an adventurous section and speaks of more freedom coming into your life so you can explore an expansive time. There is a sense of rejuvenation which flows forward out of this chapter, spending time with friends is right for your soul. Opportunity is knocking to tempt you towards a shift which brings abundance into your life. It leads to a time where you no longer have to struggle, you have a flow of advancing options which draws plenty into your world. This is an excellent brew of new potential which tempts you to rethink your trajectory and stay open to moving towards new potential. Things reached a successful conclusion soon. You are ready to make some pioneering moves. It positions you to an aspect where you can focus on expanding your horizons. You get a booster shot of adventure, as you grow your life and embrace a new vista. You are doing the right thing by being proactive and following your passions. You've never been one to be held back by fear, and you are now ready to continue an epic journey towards adventure. It leads to a goal-orientated chapter where you rethink long-term plans and merge your trajectory towards a committed situation. If you have been dealing with doubt and uncertainty, this is guiding you to expand those horizons and step out of your comfort zone.

FEBRUARY WEEK FOUR

You may just discover a shift in your attitude soon, which broadens your perceptions and sees you approach things differently. It provides you with new solutions, more balance, and a deeper understanding of how you want to move your life forward. If you have a felt you have been drifting recently, you soon reveal a more robust plan emerges. It gives you an open view of the path ahead. You have learned many painful life lessons, you have always worked so hard to achieve what you have. Tuning out distractions sees you make incredible headway on achieving those more massive dreams. You have a great deal of focus which can be channeled into goals of security. This brings you a venture which offers a room for progression, you have the talents to see it come together with a flourish. You are ready to recalibrate, rejuvenate, and renew your energy. This leads to a chapter of self-development, growth, and expansion. You zoom in on an area which offers you advancement, this does inspire a more substantial project of improving your situation. It takes you to a phase of tremendous growth, which can feel like a lot to take in. You move forward with your inner resilience and tenacity, ready to help you succeed. You can expect to sort through issues of security and uncertainty regarding your career path and embrace a way which offers room for growth. Indeed, there is a new offer arriving to tempt you towards creating a powerful shift forwards. This leads to a busy environment, it revamps your career aspect and brings a sense of fulfillment into your world as you finally can create the change you have been seeking recently. It is the fresh start you have been hoping for, allowing this potential to unfurl gently does bring you to a broad vista of inspiring possibility.

MARCH ASTROLOGY

March 2 – First Quarter Moon in Gemini.

This Moon phase occurs at 19.57 UTC.

March 9 - Full Moon in Virgo, Supermoon.

This full Moon phase occurs at 17:48 UTC. This full moon is known as the Full Worm Moon because this was the time of year when the ground would soften, and earthworms would reappear. This full moon is also known as the Full Crow Moon, the Full Crust Moon, the Full Sap Moon, and the Lenten Moon. This is also the last of four super-moons for 2020. The Moon will be closer to the Earth and will look slightly larger and brighter than usual.

March 9 - Mercury Retrograde ends in Aquarius.

You can now move forward with any delayed plans that you have been putting off due to the Mercury Retrograde phase. Relationships should soon improve as miscommunications are overcome

March 16 – Last Quarter Moon in Sagittarius.

This Moon phase occurs at 9.34 UTC. –

March 20 - March Equinox.

The March equinox takes place at 3:50 UTC. The Sun be shining on the equator, and there will be equal amounts of day and night throughout the world. This is the first day of spring (vernal equinox) in the Northern Hemisphere.

March 24 - New Moon in Aries.

The Moon is on the same side of the Earth as the Sun and will not be visible in the night sky. This phase occurs at 9:28 UTC. This is an excellent time to observe galaxies and stars because there is no moonlight to interfere.

March 24 - Mercury at most substantial Western Elongation.

The planet Mercury reaches its most substantial western elongation of 27.8 degrees from the Sun.

March 24 - Venus at most substantial Eastern Elongation.

The planet Venus reaches its most substantial Eastern elongation of 46.1 degrees from the Sun.

MARCH HOROSCOPE

MARCH WEEK ONE

If you've felt disconnected from your intuition surrounding a personal situation, you will soon gain clarity and insight into the potential possible. It will be like you're getting a triple strength vibration, a strong sense of chemistry will guide you forward. It does lead to an expansive time of following your heart and creating those big-picture goals which inspire your mind. It does bring a significant focus on interpersonal matters. There are positive signs that things are going to come together nicely for you soon. It does have you exploring new potential, you may discover a budding creative streak leads to a new enterprising venture. Getting yourself back in sync with your passion brings new options to your table. You find out yourself surrounded by plenty of supportive people who help nourish your spirit. You are ready to expand your life and follow a path which is one of high energy, it leads to a time where you are at your creative best. Everything you touch ripens, and this does help you advance your goals, it leads to a vibrant phase of being able to plot a course forward. It is a busy time, which is dynamic and sparks a new beginning for you. It reawakens your talents.

MARCH WEEK TWO

You may be feeling restless, and this can feel disorientating, it's part of a more significant theme of personal development and growth, which is seeking to emerge in your life. This is helping to open your eyes to a more mystical, spiritual side, this nourishes your spirit as it grows your gifts. It does lead to new friendships as well as an area where you can help others. There is lots of activity coming your way, this provides you with plenty of gratitude and good cheer. It ignites incredible potential which allows you reconnect with a more social environment. There is also some exciting communication coming, which brings exciting, long-awaited news. You share an open dialogue with another, which is a significant turning point. You have been doing a fantastic job of creating a healing environment, if you have found yourself struggling to let go of old patterns, or are dealing with self-doubt, you can feel proud of the work you are doing. It does connect you to a lighted chapter where you can process these emotions, a creative venture is also therapeutic, this enables you to pick up speed and embrace a new flow of energy which arrives to shift your focus forward. This is a great time to plot a course towards the achievement of an important goal. You can expect the emergence of inspiration and motivation to help create the shift needed to get the ball rolling on a new chapter of potential. In fact, it's a time where you set your sights on a bigger picture vision, it inspires you to expand your limits.

MARCH WEEK THREE

It is a time of turning inwards and reflecting on past events. You have been through a time of change, perhaps the situation did not reach its full potential, and you are left trying to grasp the complexities of the case, and what went wrong. There are a few twists and turns ahead to navigate, but it does lead to a favorable aspect to where you can unite with your love interest in perfect harmony. You experience a breakthrough around your life, this provides you with a long-term option, and it does light up a path where you can appreciate a wealth of opportunities which arrive to support nurturing a serious bond. It is a bold time which sees you embrace life. It is a potent time which leads to an enriching phase where you can plot a course towards developing longer-term goals. Any minor issues around bickering or miscommunication should resolve quickly. There is a flow of harmony and abundance, which is supporting a phase of growth. This suggests that you are going to make headway on deepening a bond which offers a great deal of room to progress further. Looking ahead you face a crossroads where you do make a decision where you advance down a particular direction, it does suggest taking time to contemplate your options is essential, you don't want to have to go through the same drama again. Putting an emphasis on your goals and dreams to help you advocate for the right direction. It's time, which brings endings, transitions, and closure.

MARCH WEEK FOUR

Slowing your situation down enables you to tackle one case at a time. You will likely receive new information soon, which helps you plot a course towards a beneficial environment. You may feel under pressure during these challenging conditions, but this is where the most exceptional growth occurs. Something good is going to come out of this time of tension. Your resilience and tenacity are growing to support a solution. You are headed towards a more positive chapter, this gives you a nudge in the right direction, it enables you to embark on expanding your horizons and following your dreams. Knowing you have the support of your closest ties, gives you the green light to embrace a happier future. You are more than ready to create change in your life, this enables you to focus on achieving those larger goals. It does set the stage for a shift towards significant growth. Building a stable foundation does become a priority. It leads to a time of achieving a stellar result. You are transforming your life and will soon advance your situation. Fundamental changes occur which enable you to move towards an area of interest. You set your creative energies free on achieving a goal. A solution arrives, and a shift forward occurs in quick succession. It all leads to the achievement of a beautiful result. This sees you embrace a happy chapter ahead. News should arrive soon. You are being supported to push back the barriers which constrict your life, this leads to an extraordinary expansion, it has you taking a leap of faith towards achieving those larger emotional goals. It is an ideal time to focus on setting intentions, looking at your options, you find you can create space for something new to flow into your world. It does bring a bounty of options to your table to explore.

APRIL ASTROLOGY

April 1 – First Quarter Moon in Cancer.

This Moon phase occurs at 10.21 UTC.

April 8 - Full Moon in Libra, Supermoon.

The Moon is on the opposite side of the Earth as the Sun and will be completely illuminated. This moon phase occurs at 2:35 UTC. This full moon is known as Full Pink Moon because it marked an appearance of the first spring flowers. This full moon has also been identified as the Sprouting Grass Moon, the Growing Moon, and the Egg Moon. Many coastal areas call it Full Fish Moon because this was the time the fish swam upriver to breed.

April 14 – Last Quarter Moon in Capricorn.

This Moon phase occurs at 22.56 UTC.

April 22, 23 - Lyrids Meteor Shower.

The Lyrids meteor shower runs each year from April 16-25. This meteor shower peaks on the night of the 22nd and the morning of the 23rd. These meteors sometimes produce blazing dust trails that last for several seconds.

April 23 - New Moon in Taurus.

The New Moon is on the same side of the Earth as the Sun and will not be visible in the night sky. This moon phase occurs at 2:26 UTC. This is an excellent time to observe galaxies and stars because there is no moonlight visible.

April 30 – First Quarter Moon in Leo.

This Moon phase occurs at 20.38 UTC.

APRIL HOROSCOPE

APRIL WEEK ONE

You are on the tail end of a phase which has been significant, it has led to a more extended time of personal growth, which will provide you with crucial benefits in the chapter ahead. Once you move your energy forward towards a time which draws abundance and happiness into your life, you can look in the rearview vision mirror and say goodbye to any struggles you are currently dealing with. You are transitioning to a new aspect, this can feel unsettling as it shakes up your environment, it creates energetic vibrations which lift your thoughts, it creates growth as you begin to focus more on personal development. It does unite your situation by creating the right environment for you to make a breakthrough around your long-term goals. News arrives, which lights up your mind with new inspiration. This week is one of abundance, the future shimmers brightly with new potential. Impulse sweeps in to encourage you to keep the rewards of expanding your horizons. It does offer you possibilities which create significant change, it leads to a more abundant and happier way of life. This is something you have been looking for some time, and you can enjoy the rewards this week brings. It is a time where you can cultivate closer bonds, any inspiring initiatives launched surrounding these ties does help unite a more intimate situation with people you care about. In fact, there is a celebration ahead which enables a sense of rejuvenation to occur, if a relationship has felt sensitive, you will be able to embrace a new-found flow of healing energy which sees a stronger bond emerge from this renewal.

APRIL WEEK TWO

You will be recognized soon for some of your excellent work. It may further your course to become more involved in social justice. While it takes time to navigate the right path, which suits your current situation, there is lighthearted energy arriving to tempt you towards expansion. This essential shift is helping to heal aspects which have hindered progress recently. You can initiate changes which bring good fortune, taking time to contemplate the options does open an avenue currently hidden. Keep your mind open, something is on the way which helps you pitch a grand plan towards growth. This leads to a thought-provoking time as fresh ideas inspire your soul. You are going through a transformational phase which reshapes your priorities, possibly even your entire identity. It is a time of rejuvenation and evolution for you on many levels. It helps you rebuild your life to match your current goals and visions. There are areas you have outgrown, while a restless vibe has you wanting to bring new excitement into your life. You are journeying towards an expansive chapter. It does see the reemergence of people you haven't seen for a while, this can rattle your emotional sensitivities, as you are faced with looking back to past events. Taking time to set boundaries helps to ground and reestablish your vision. It does see you circulating in a more social environment soon. You enter a more social time, and this sees you spending time with your social set. It does bring invitations to circulate and leads to a lighthearted chapter, it heightens your human spirit, and provides you with a rich source of inspiration and rejuvenation. You may feel tempted to start exploring opportunities in your wider community, which has you cross the path of a kindred spirit who complements your life.

APRIL WEEK THREE

Like a tree that is nourished, you depend on a secure environment to thrive. Touching base with your family does help you take a nostalgic trip down memory lane. This nurtures family bonds it draws emotional healing into your life. Nurturing your environment creates a wellspring of abundance. It also seems you are ready to start crafting your visions into something inspiring. You initiate changes which overhaul your life and create a shift forward. It leads to a more sustainable environment, one which suits your freedom loving and expansive mind. It does bring a rare opportunity to expand your talents into a new area. This opens an avenue which is expressive, exciting, and creative. You harness your gifts and set off on a new adventure which brings blessings. The past has been a time of growth and wisdom. It has created a mix of fortunes, which have given you a journey well worth contemplating. Currently, you feel ready to honor a quiet part of your soul. This suggests a trip inward, and you explore options which focus on self-development and nurturing a hidden aspect of your spirit. You have gifts and talents ready to be revealed in the coming chapter. Several options are arriving to tempt you towards growth. It does highlight information coming, which opens an avenue to explore. This is a sign that you are ready to grow your talents, it helps you release lingering doubts and brings a challenge worthy of your attention. You can gain traction on a bigger vision and feel motivated and productive in the workplace. Your efforts gain momentum, your diligence may be rewarded with a new role. You have a good head on your shoulders for business. There are gifts and talents ready to reach the light of day, focusing on a strategy and plan to achieve your goals will pay dividends in the coming chapter.

APRIL WEEK FOUR

The future is looking bright, there is something in the pipeline which provides you with a wonderful sense of security. This provides you with a stable platform, it's from these foundations you can grow your broader career goals. Advancement is looming, it takes you towards a time of hectic activity. It can feel like pressure at first, but it is the best way to grow your potential in the workplace. Unusual changes are in the pipeline, which enables you to focus on creating a bridge from your current situation towards a happier chapter. It is part of a larger cycle of growth which is calling you to expand your talents. Following your dreams does set in motion a remarkable chain of events which enable you to make progress on a solid phase of growth. It does lead to an exciting reveal soon. There is a sense that you have a great deal of potential set to unfold in your world. It does lead to a happy chapter where you can expand your life and embrace a new flow of energy. Finding the right path for your gifts is key to making the most of this essential time. Information is coming, which helps guide you forward towards an active phase of potential. A situation you nurture does blossom into a meaningful bond. It brings a great deal of abundance into your life and does set the stage for a lovely phase of growth. Sharing time with this person brings a great deal of positivity into your life. It is a beautiful foundation to grow a bond.

MAY ASTROLOGY

May 6, 7 - Eta Aquarids Meteor Shower.

The Eta Aquarids meteor shower runs annually from April 19 to May 28. It peaks this year on the night of May 6 and the morning of May 7.

May 7 - Full Moon in Scorpio, Supermoon.

The Moon is on the opposite side of the Earth as the Sun, and its face will be fully illuminated. This phase occurs at 10:45 UTC. The May full moon is known as the Full Flower Moon because this was the time of year when spring flowers are in abundance. This full moon is also known as the Full Corn Planting Moon and the Milk Moon. This is also the last of four supermoons for 2020. The Moon will be at its closest approach to the Earth and looks slightly larger and brighter.

May 14 – Last Quarter Moon in Aquarius.

This Moon phase occurs at 14.03 UTC.

May 22 - New Moon in Taurus.

The Moon will be located on the same side of the Earth as the Sun and won't be seen in the night sky. This phase occurs at 17:39 UTC. The new moon phase is a brilliant time to observe galaxies and stars because there is no moonlight visible.

May 30 – First Quarter Moon in Virgo.

This Moon phase occurs at 3.30 UTC.

MAY HOROSCOPE

MAY WEEK ONE

This is an energizing time, the May 7th Supermoon leaves you feeling especially uplifted. You are ready to grow your talents, and this leads to an exciting time. A flurry of activity arrives to tempt you towards growth. You discover a project to put on the front burner, it could lead to a significant turning point. Advocating for your dreams is the way to go. No more waiting, you can go for it. You are ready to investigate new opportunities. Any uncertainty you feel about moving out of your comfort zone can be pushed back and released. You are prepared to emerge into a more social environment, this energy simmers and percolates, creating a fantastic brew of potential for you to explore. You focus on well-being and getting things back on track. An offer arrives, which brings new information, it gives you a burst of motivation and creates an alignment towards a chapter worth exploring. This helps you turn a clean page over and start fresh. You kick off a fresh episode in your life soon. This ignites new energy, as you ground and center your energy, you invite a sanctuary of healing into your life, which further grows your goals. There is plenty to look forward to in the chapter ahead. The sun shines brightly over your world, clear skies emerge to tempt you towards expanding your horizons. There is a sense of being able to dial down commitments, simplify, and get your life back into a steadier groove. Pacing your self enables you to integrate the fast flowing energy, which is set to arrive soon. It does lead to a bustling social aspect. Directing your thoughts with intention does bring positive outcomes for your life.

MAY WEEK TWO

It is a time which is restorative, you untangle negative aspects, and areas which have hindered your progress. Feelings are coming up which are healing the past, it does help you wrap up that chapter, and release it once and for all. You can soon welcome in fresh energy with exuberance and excitement, doing the necessary healing leaves you feeling energized, it leads to a more creatively spontaneous chapter, one where you usher in new potential, and this lights a lovely path forward towards a brighter environment. You are ready to create positive change, against a stormy backdrop which has been emotionally intense, transformation occurs, taking your potential towards a closer romantic situation. It does see various elements come together to bring your life the harmony you have been seeking. This involves processing heavy emotions, and it does see a deep connection being forged, which brings you joy. You have been through a time of upheaval, this forces you to completely reset your life trajectory. While it has been difficult for you to find your groove, it has enabled you to discover new parts of your identity, and this has led to a great deal of personal growth. It does take you to a passionate original path, one where you can create a bond which offers a deep sense of connection. It helps you build a stable foundation from which to grow. You may be feeling unsettled or restless, and this is part of a larger cycle of growth you are in, which is calling you to increase your spiritual side. It is an awakening, where you can open your eyes to a new area, this calling is highly therapeutic, it heals aspects of your spirit, which have been injured in the past. Drawing abundance and well-being into your core foundational element is highly beneficial.

MAY WEEK THREE

This week leads to a powerful chapter where your intuition does become heightened, it could bring moments of intense déjà vu, which may be disorientating. This energy is spiritually productive and can help you manifest a more balanced and soulful environment. It does heighten your emotional wellness as it grounds you in a phase which offers to heal as well as illuminating new ideas to explore. There is excitement ahead as the future brings a bold new beginning into your world. It does see news or a vital decision arriving, this creates a lifestyle change, it revamps your situation, and can significantly help you as it inspires you to begin a new area. This endeavor connects you with excellent times, it has you thinking about the previous chapter and could position you for better opportunities to soon follow. It touches you down on a branch which revamps the possibilities available to you, reshuffling and balancing your aspirations, you veer towards a situation which is enticing, and reveals a substantial potential is possible. This prompts you to tread carefully, as it does bring with it a sense of excitement. There are options available to expand your horizons and brushing up on your creative talents do lead to an expansive chapter. It has a beautiful ability to put you in contact with a more extensive social set of like-minded individuals. Spending time in a group environment not only feeds your mind, but it also nurtures your spirit.

MAY WEEK FOUR

There may be a lack of closure in your life, which is limiting progress. Spending time reflecting on the past, and the ways that it shaped your present situation is therapeutic. Creating a healing environment, and this can be done in many ways. Lighting a candle with intention, self-care with spending time nurturing your spirit, or just creating space to do this inner work. You are someone who gives a lot to other people in your life. You are dependable and have an excellent ability to nurture others. The special touch you give to projects and people you care about is a beautiful talent. It connects you with a more considerable capacity to heal areas which are often neglected. It enables you to be a source of guidance and assistance, a right gift, indeed. You are a wonderful person who brings a lot of joy to others in your life. A groundbreaking chapter is coming, which holds game-changing potential. You are ready to take on the world and enter into a solid phase of growth and advancement. Little breaks your stride as you harness a sense of determination to succeed. Taking time for yourself helps to recalibrate your energy, it creates a lovely shift where you can pause and renew your potential. It does heal aspects which have been holding you back, as you release areas which no longer serve your higher purpose, you discover a new flow of inspiration flows into your life to keep the momentum facing forward. This brings you to a lighter and happier chapter.

JUNE ASTROLOGY

June 4 - Mercury at Greatest Eastern Elongation.

The planet Mercury reaches greatest eastern elongation of 23.6 degrees from the Sun.

June 5 - Full Moon in Sagittarius.

The Full Moon is on the opposite side of the Earth as the Sun, and its face will be completely illuminated. This moon phase occurs at 19:12 UTC. This full moon is known as Full Strawberry Moon because it is the peak of the strawberry harvesting season. The June Full Moon has also been identified as the Full Rose Moon and the Full Honey Moon.

June 5 – Penumbral Lunar Eclipse.

This Moon eclipse occurs when the Moon passes through the Earth's partial shadow or penumbra. During this type of eclipse, the Moon will darken slightly but not completely disappear. This lunar eclipse will be visible throughout most of Europe, Africa, Asia, and Australia.

June 10 - Jupiter at Opposition.

The planet Jupiter will be at its nearest approach to Earth, and its planet face will be illuminated entirely by the Sun.

June 13 – Last Quarter Moon in Pisces.

This Moon phase occurs at 6.24 UTC.

June 17 – Mercury Retrograde begins in Cancer.

During a retrograde period, it isn't the right time to move forward in any practical venture. Be prepared for misunderstandings and miscommunications to be prevalent.

June 21 - June Solstice.

The June solstice occurs at 21:44 UTC. The North Pole will be tilted toward the Sun, which, having reached its northernmost position in the sky will be over the Tropic of Cancer at 23.44 degrees north latitude. This heralds the first day of summer (summer solstice) in the Northern Hemisphere, and is considered one of the most critical times of the year for many traditional cultures. It is the first day of winter (winter solstice) for the Southern Hemisphere.

June 21 - New Moon in Cancer.

The Moon is on the same side of the Earth as the Sun and will not be visible in the night sky. This moon phase occurs at 6:41 UTC. This is an excellent time to observe galaxies and stars because there is little moonlight to obstruct your view.

June 21 – Annual Solar Eclipse.

An annular solar eclipse occurs when the Moon is too far away from the Earth to completely cover the Sun. This results in a ring of light around the darkened Moon. The Sun's corona is not visible during an annular eclipse. The path of this solar eclipse begins in central Africa and travel through Saudi Arabia, northern India, and southern China before ending in the Pacific Ocean. A partial solar eclipse occurs throughout most of eastern Africa, the Middle East, and South Asia.

June 28 – First Quarter Moon in Libra.

This Moon phase occurs at 8.16 UTC.

JUNE HOROSCOPE

JUNE WEEK ONE

A myriad of options to further grow creative talents are arriving soon, this provides you with a beautiful path which offers room for progression. It expands your life and gives back to others. You have the skills to make this venture a rousing success. The attention to detail and your willingness to uncover the potential fully will provide you with ample rewards. It does suggest a meticulous approach is needed, and this will bring you an active phase of growth. You do shift to a stage which sparkles with fantastic potential. It does create the ability to radically improve your situation. It turns a new page over, and this fresh start is just the beginning. As you begin to see tangible results, you become more inspired to continue to reveal the full potential possible. It does help you deal with hurdles, and this gears you up for a more extensive phase of expansion. Doing your due diligence will enable you to take appropriate steps to build the right foundations with this opportunity. Having necessary safeguards allow you to make the most of this potential. It does lead to productive times, hard work, and perseverance can really increase your chances of a successful outcome. Having a goal to focus on enables an environment which is inspired and motivated. You enter a productive chapter which offers opportunities to network, it connects you with a broader world of potential, you create space to engage in areas which bring you joy. A lot is happening where you can discover areas of growth, it leads to an exciting time which blesses you with invitations and events. Surprise news ahead leads to a lovely celebration with kindred folk.

JUNE WEEK TWO

The planet Jupiter reaches its closest approach to the earth this week. It will be at its brightest, and this illuminates a new direction. Jupiters influence is one of luck, expansion, and good fortune. Some upgrades are coming into your life soon. Some curious changes are unfolding, which may bring exciting news soon. It leads to a productive chapter which enables you to connect with high-level options. This positions you favorably to enjoy a phase which features growth and expansion. Honing up on your talents does make the most of this exciting chapter. This is a creative time for you, you feel more imaginative, it does draw new ideas into your world for a reason. It sees a project of importance feature prominently in your life soon. Focusing on developing this potential leads to a phase of growth. This advances your situation and draws further options into your world. This is an exciting time that brings joy.

Furthermore, broadening your perception, you discover ways to streamline spending, becoming more efficient overall does have a benefit of improving your situation. It helps you resolve issues and gives you a preview of a positive chapter, which is coming soon. It pairs you with a path that draws abundance into your world. You are heading toward a time where you can improve your situation. Utilizing elements of strategy brings a considerable spike of potential into your life, this influence is fortuitous and could yield some impressive results. There fantastic opportunities available should you invest your energy in uncovering this potential. It does lead to an expansive chapter where you brush up on your skills, and this provides tangible results.

JUNE WEEK THREE

The June 21st Solstice is an ideal time to pause and reflect on your goals. A memorable life event coming soon. You can maneuver forward and embrace the changes ahead. It does bring you viable options to consider. This sees partnering with a new area that draws excitement into your life. It matches your talents with an area that has room for progression. As your creativity flourishes, you discover an innovative option worth developing. You cross the path of an individual whose looks are striking. This person is a bit of a mystery. At first, they take time to get to know, but starting with a friendship first does give you room to deepen the bond gently. It leads to a time which inspires and brings a beautiful sense of excitement into your life. It does take you to a chapter which offers you many blessings, as this person brings you joy. New options arriving for you soon. The fact that this is a bit of a mystery only heightens a sense of excitement. It does show the outcomes are positive, it takes you to a path where you can harness a strong sense of vision. This is highly creative, and your mind helps to inspire growth by spending time brainstorming ideas with people who understand your goals. An event crops up where you get a chance to celebrate with friends and family. It does bring a wonderful sense of abundance into your world. The people present are very enthusiastic and happy about what is happening. It's clearly the culmination of a long journey, and indeed, it does bring you joy.

JUNE WEEK FOUR

Mercury Retrograde sees an interpersonal bond misfiring due to differences of opinion, the timing isn't the best, and miscommunication has limited progress. New potential arrives after July 12th to shake the situation up, and it does provide opportunities to nurture this bond in a more fertile environment. This leads to expanded opportunities with this character, it brings positive energy to your landscape. There is a beautiful phase coming, which enables you to create space for something inspiring to arrive. It does bring you to a chapter which rings especially true, it connects with a passion of yours, and does enable you to make those changes happen which bring abundance into your life. The process of putting yourself first is an essential step in drawing new options into your life. You have been taking on a lot recently, and it is up an excellent time for you to seek balance, to look at a bigger picture, and nurture your spirit. That which surrounds your life will unfold in due course, you can't control everything. You can take care of yourself, and this has a beneficial ripple effect which helps others in your circle. You have abilities to overcome challenges, your resilience inspires others. An open door comes in your life, which offers new opportunities, you discover things turn out better than anticipated, and this provides you with expanded options soon. You may have been going through some adjustments, but you will later see that these changes were necessary and do lead to improvement further down the track. It is natural to resist change, but you are evolving, growing your spirit, and this will lead to heighten self-expression, which draws abundance into your life.

JULY ASTROLOGY

July 5 - Full Moon in Capricorn.

The July Full Moon is located on the opposite side of the Earth as the Sun and will be fully illuminated. This phase occurs at 4:44 UTC. This full moon is known as Full Buck Moon because the male buck deer start to grow new antlers. This full moon is also known as the Full Thunder Moon and the Full Hay Moon.

July 5 – Penumbral Lunar Eclipse.

This Moon eclipse occurs when the Moon passes through the Earth's partial shadow or penumbra. During this type of eclipse, the Moon will darken slightly but not completely disappear. This lunar eclipse will be visible throughout most of Europe, Africa, Asia, and Australia.

July 12 – Last Quarter Moon in Aries.

This Moon phase occurs at 23.29 UTC.

July 12 - Mercury Retrograde ends in Cancer.

You can now move forward with any delayed plans that you have been putting off due to the Mercury Retrograde phase. Relationships should soon improve as communication improves.

July 14 - Jupiter at Opposition.

The Giant planet Jupiter will be at its nearest approach to Earth and will be at it's brightest.

July 20 - New Moon in Cancer.

The July New Moon is located on the same side of the Earth as the Sun and won't be visible in the night sky. This moon phase occurs at 17:33 UTC. This is an excellent time to observe galaxies and stars because there is no moonlight visible.

July 20 - Saturn at Opposition.

The beautiful ringed planet Saturn will be at its nearest approach to Earth and will be illuminated by the Sun.

July 22 - Mercury at Greatest Western Elongation.

The planet Mercury reaches greatest western elongation of 20.1 degrees from the Sun.

July 27 – First Quarter Moon in Scorpio.

This Moon phase occurs at 12.32 UTC.

July 28, 29 - Delta Aquarids Meteor Shower.

The Delta Aquarids meteor shower peaks on the night of July 28 and morning of July 29. The first quarter moon may block many of the fainter meteors this year. You should still be able to view the brighter ones. Best viewing will be at a dark vista after midnight. Meteors radiate from the constellation Aquarius but can appear anywhere in the sky.

JULY HOROSCOPE

JULY WEEK ONE

The full moon this week connects you to your intuition and higher wisdom. Your subconscious keeps track, it does weigh down your energy, doing healing work is vital, it sends a strong message that you are ready to let go and move forward. You dare to face the past and acknowledge that it no longer has a hold over you. This emphasizes that you have shut the door on a chapter which was ingrained in your spirit more than you care to admit. A fresh chapter awaits an open heart. If you have felt restricted or stuck recently, there is a powerful shift which sees a new option open. It does have you feeling more optimistic, and gives you a better idea of the direction you are heading towards. This gives you a better ability to handle any delays which have limited progress. A shift forward brings change, and you welcome the improvement, which soon follows. You discover a situation needs reworking, it turns out to be a blessing in disguise. Looking at the situation from a new perspective enables you to light up a better solution. This brings you to a chapter where you create space to nurture your creative side. It does see you spending more time on areas which inspire your mind. You discover your priorities are shifting, and this draws harmony into your life. There may be an area which is confusing for you at this time, it is best not to rush into anything, and look at all the available information so that you can reach an informed decision. Making the correct choice does give you options to expand your life, and draw a new area into being. It is a great time, and while it may see one chapter closing, a fresh flow of opportunities soon arrive.

JULY WEEK TWO

Mercury Retrograde ends on the 12th of July, and this sees you successfully emerge from a cocoon where you have sheltered your creativity recently. There is something around the corner for you, it is the beginning of a fresh start. It does bring news which may take a moment to assimilate as you realize your search is over. It does expand your options, and this brings a wonderful sense of potential into your world. You have persevered and been on a long journey, soon you will get the offer which brightens your day. You get a clue about the direction you are headed in more quickly, this clarity does open a path forward. Your fortunes are rising, and this leads to more freedom, a chapter emerges where you can embrace a higher sense of self-expression and creativity. The problem is, you're not currently where you want to be now, and this can leave you feeling frustrated and despondent. Focus on the plan, a shift forward is coming. You have big ideas, yet it's challenging to know how to put your dreams into action. It does bring difficulties, which need to be surmounted before you can truly expand your horizons. There is an alternative method, taking small steps to help create a more extensive change, which overall benefits your situation. Adaptability and flexibility in good measure enable you to piece the jigsaw together.

JULY WEEK THREE

You discover a new angle which enables you to head for gold soon. Despite difficulties which have impeded progress recently, you ply an original approach, your insistence leads to excellence. Your qualities shine brightly, and this elevates your potential, it transforms your situation, and may even lead to a breakthrough moment soon. The important news is coming, which puts an emphasis on obtaining a stellar result. You are serious about improving your fortune, unique benefits arrive in the form of a collaborative approach, support is available, teaming up with someone who offers practical advice does enable you to find alternative solutions to problems which have prevented progress. Challenges are not insurmountable if you harness the right outlook, tenacity, and resilience are on the rise, leading to the optimal environment for growth. Changes in the source of your income enable you to stay ahead of the game. It does put you in the box seat to take advantage of a new flow of energy, this may see you change jobs, and score a new role. There are many benefits likely to come from this transformation, you are headed towards a chapter which emphasizes growth, it beautifully positions you to take advantage of an offer which crops up soon. Giving yourself time to reflect on the options available to you will help you generate the ideas needed to improve your circumstances. It does see a boost to your situation, your creativity is ahead of the game. It enables you to journey towards an area where you can put action into play. This edges you closer to achieving a substantial goal. You discover a path opens which offers room for progression.

JULY WEEK FOUR

You have creative abilities which are likely to be further revealed over time. There are incredible ways to grow your talents, and exploring your options will help guide you to areas which inspire and motivate you to hone your skills. You have a unique flare, and this artistic ability enables you to shine. You discover a new chapter can be launched. You finally can share your talents with a broader audience. Focusing on the path forward, you listen to your intuition, and find strength and stability amid the shift forward which takes place. It is an especially potent time for self-development, you discover an opportunity to explore a little worn path which speaks to your spirit. You are creating positive change which impacts those around you. This ripple effect of positive vibrations to bring a wonderful sense of abundance into your life. A new path is calling, which offers room for growth. As you move forward, you discover a new area becomes a priority. It does see you going the extra mile to achieve the outcome you desire. Your focused attention does win out, and this area becomes fruitful. It does lead to a time which brings good fortune and potential into your world. Life becomes vibrant as you discover attractive opportunities to circulate in a more full social environment. You have had some ups and downs recently, and there is support available, letting another person help does draw abundance into your life. Widening your view stimulates creative thinking and brings new options to your table. There is plenty of fun ahead, and this broadens the scope of your life and brings you in contact with a new friendship or two. Additionally, a welcome surprise arrives soon.

AUGUST ASTROLOGY

August 3 - Full Moon in Aquarius.

The August Full Moon is located on the opposite side of the Earth as the Sun and will be fully illuminated. This phase occurs at 15:59 UTC. The August full moon is known as the Full Sturgeon Moon because sturgeon fish of the Great Lakes and other major lakes were quickly caught during this time. This full moon has also been known as the Green Corn Moon and the Grain Moon.

August 11 – Last Quarter Moon in Taurus.

This Moon phase occurs at 16.45 UTC.

August 12, 13 - Perseids Meteor Shower.

The Perseids meteor shower runs each year from July 17 to August 24. It peaks this year on the night of August 12 and the morning of August 13. The Perseids meteor shower is one of the best to view as the meteors are so bright and numerous. The best viewing is from a dark vista after midnight.

August 13 - Venus at Greatest Western Elongation.

The planet Venus reaches greatest western elongation of 45.8 degrees from the Sun.

August 19 - New Moon in Leo.

The Moon will be on the same side of the Earth as the Sun and will not be visible in the night sky. This moon phase occurs at 2:41 UTC. This is an excellent time to observe galaxies and stars because there is no moonlight to obstruct the view.

August 25 – First Quarter Moon in Scorpio.

This Moon phase occurs at 17.58 UTC.

AUGUST HOROSCOPE

AUGUST WEEK ONE

The road ahead does take planning, you may discover that it requires greater flexibility and adjustment to achieve rapid growth. Negotiating the path ahead could lead to tension, it also triggers changes around your career goals. Reshuffling your options enables you to streamline your situation and align your way correctly. Tangible results soon follow. Fortunes ebb and flow, if you feel lower then you would like, it's good to focus on balance and rejuvenation. You have taken a lot on board recently, and now it is time to integrate these changes into your life so that you can move forward stably and securely. This brings positive energy into your landscape, it allows you to acknowledge higher aspects of life which bring blessings into your world. You are ready for a new direction, this is a chapter which culminates in the sense of closure, as you shut the door on an area which feels done with. Once you have the past out of vision, you create space for a new path to inspire change. It does bring good news, and this offers you a chance to put your talents to the test in a highly creative fashion. It emphasizes an exciting chapter of levity and adventure arrives. You can expect change to flow into your world soon. This sweeps in an environment which is conducive to growth, it puts goals front and center for you to develop. You are ready to create space for something new, and you have the abilities to make the most of this groundbreaking chapter. Your creativity is a dramatic tool to create the changes required to improve your situation.

AUGUST WEEK TWO

You are in a reflective cycle which helps you get in touch with your intuition, it enables you to gain access to your higher goals, this gives you opportunities to visualize a path which draws abundance into your life. Listening to your gut instincts will be especially powerful, it does help you break free of doubt and confusion. It may even connect you with a substantial goal to develop soon. You enter a phase where blockages are released, it does create space for positive energy to rejuvenate and renew your spirit. A gateway opens dramatically to a future path which you can explore and enjoy an exciting chapter of refreshing possibilities. You sweep aside limitations as these are only hindrances, which limit your ability to achieve your important goals. The exciting potential is growing in the background of your awareness. You may feel confused about your life's direction, you have been through unpredictable times, careful consideration does help you plan a path which is stable and secure. An opportunity on the horizon lets you feel more grounded. Honoring your emotional side does give you a sanctuary from the hectic pace of life. This buffer zone is an area which you will return to when life is feeling chaotic or draining. It's a powerful tool of rejuvenation. Revolution is possible and leads to a compelling outcome in your life. It helps you draw harmony and happiness into your world because you filter out distractions and go after an important goal you have set for yourself. It begins a voyage filled with promise, a big reveal arrives, which sparks your curiosity and inspires your mind. It is a shift which enables you to head towards freedom and expansion.

AUGUST WEEK THREE

You have gifts ready to emerge, you begin to see your capabilities in a new light, it does enable you to resonate on a higher level and plot a course which is expressive and creative. You discover surprising help arrives, which allows you to build a closer friendship with one who had fallen by the wayside in the past. This person becomes a sounding board for you to share thoughts and ideas with. You are entering a social chapter which enables you to pick up the thread of a friendship which had been fraying. This sees a closer bond emerging, and it does invite happy moments into your world. As the alliance improves, you are allowed to build a venture together, a collaborative approach does enable swifter growth to occur. It invites abundance into your world. The fantastic news is arriving soon, which gives you a chance to improve your situation. It gives you a direct link where you can focus on achieving a home-based goal. It does draw opportunities to participate in a community setting as well. It is a time of new information, big moves, and planning for future growth. A moment of kindness from a friend leads to an invitation out with others. There is lighthearted energy arriving, it does offer a sense of fun and excitement. Situations which felt complicated and problematic can suddenly be resolved with a sudden eureka moment. As you break through towards a more abundant phase, you can harness powerful opportunities to head towards growth. Expect Swift news to arrive a which sets you in a new direction, this fresh start is revolutionary.

AUGUST WEEK FOUR

You have had obstacles to navigate, but rest assured, things are set to improve soon. Taking adequate measures to plot a course does protect your potential on all levels. A plan in place prevents possible misfires, it takes you towards a chapter where you can make progress on your career. You may have had some frustrations with your job this year, this is set to change. There is stabilizing energy reaching you soon, it helps you bring the balance back into your life, as this grounds your power you can be open to a creative chapter which has you open a new path potential. You think outside of the box, this sees you taking an innovative approach to a goal or other area of your life you have been trying to improve recently. Focus on one aspect at a time is the best. You battle some issues which impede your progress. It can feel like an uphill battle. Insight and clarity are available, which will begin a journey towards improving your situation. It can feel like a double-edged sword at times, but you are moving towards the opportunities which come knocking. A new chapter is beginning, and you gain insight into the path ahead by utilizing focused energy, which turns inward and allows you to access regions of the mind often hidden from you. This is a time of finding quiet contemplation and of being able to listen to your inner voice without distractions overriding the message. It is a time of waiting to hear news or developments.

SEPTEMBER ASTROLOGY

September 2 - Full Moon in Pisces.

The September full Moon is on the opposite side of the Earth as the Sun, and its face will be fully illuminated. This phase occurs at 5:22 UTC. This full moon is known as the Full Corn Moon because the corn is harvested around this time.

September 10 – Last Quarter Moon in Gemini.

This Moon phase occurs at 9.26 UTC.

September 11 - Neptune at Opposition.

The giant blue planet will be at its closest approach to Earth, and its face will be illuminated by the Sun.

September 17 - New Moon in Virgo.

The Moon is on the same side of the Earth as the Sun and will not be visible in the night sky. This phase occurs at 11:00 UTC. This is an excellent time to observe galaxies and stars because there is no moonlight visible.

September 22 - September Equinox.

The 2020 September equinox occurs at 13:31 UTC. The Sun shines directly on the equator, creating equal amounts of day and night throughout the world. This is also the first day of fall (autumnal equinox) in the northern hemisphere and is considered a significant zodiac event for many traditional cultures.

September 24 – First Quarter Moon in Capricorn.

This Moon phase occurs at 1.55 UTC.

SEPTEMBER HOROSCOPE

SEPTEMBER WEEK ONE

You can expand your horizons and get involved in an area which draws abundance into your world. This has a powerful influence over your emotional awareness, there is inspiration coming, it does see your organizational skills, and other creative talents put to good use. It is a fantastic chapter where you give something back, and this is a rewarding and inspiring path for you to take. It does lead to an exceptional episode where little breaks your stride. As you make your big push forward, you discover that life supports a vision of movement and vitality. It has you viewing your situation in a new light, this gives you new options to explore, and beautiful developments enable speedy growth. This heightens productivity, and you resonate an aura which is hectic and lively. You bring a sweet opportunity into your life that blends well with your current situation, it brings changes which benefits your life, there is an emphasis on developing a personal bond which is highly inspiring, it motivates you to take significant interest in planning for future growth. It eclipses the pain of the past with golden sunshine, which beams into your life. It does draw abundance and joy. This is an ideal time to circulate in your wider community, you cross the path of someone who later becomes a friend, this lucky coincidence sets the stage for some essential changes which help shape a chapter further down the line. It is a time of inspiration and sunny skies which draw abundance into your life. Surprise news arrives to have you thinking big about future prospects.

SEPTEMBER WEEK TWO

The planet Neptune is at its closest approach to Earth this week, it will be at its brightest. Neptune rules your house of dreams and healing. If you have been feeling overwhelmed or drained recently, you can expect a new flow of energy to arrive, which helps open the path ahead towards a more vibrant and energetic chapter. This resonates positively with you and enables you to create space to explore creative options. It sets the stage for you to amplify your goals and create tangible progress, which is beneficial for your life. Your talents are on the rise, as this happy trend emerges in your life, it sets the tone for a fun and exciting chapter where you can nurture your creative talents, and explore developing your intuitive gifts. There are attractive options open which offer you a chance to mingle in a broader social environment with kindred spirits who share your passion for the mystical arts. An offer crosses your path which tempts you towards expansion soon. There may be a few adjustments coming up, overall, positive changes are arriving. It does bring news to the surface, which is relevant to your situation, it governs your ability to plot a path towards future growth. This enables you to reboot your potential and refocus your energy to provide you with the highest potential possible. This is not a time for complacency, new methods and pathways are calling your name. You enter a chapter soon, which eclipses anything that has gone before. It does see a higher vibration emerging in your world, which is hugely motivating and inspiring. This leads to an exciting chapter where you can achieve stellar outcomes by following the passion within your heart. It is an ideal time to emerge from your cocoon and take in some bold moves forward.

SEPTEMBER WEEK THREE

This week could bring a significant change for you, it sweeps away old energy, removes limitations and blockages, and enables you to create space for a compelling chapter of growth to emerge. This brings new opportunities, it clarifies your goals and brings exciting options to your table. This is an auspicious time which draws luck and good fortune into your life. It does enable you to shine and make the best use of your talents. It is a dynamic time which sees new options flow quickly into your life, this gives you steppingstones towards achieving those essential dreams and goals you often have on the back burner. Your situation is transforming towards a focused chapter where you can utilize a heightened flow of potential which arrives to instigate a phase of growth. Your vision of future goals is undergoing essential changes, it is evolving and taking you on a substantial path where you can take in lofty sights and set the bar higher for what you hope to achieve. A shift is coming where you re-balance your life and explore a phase of self-expression through utilizing creativity and vision. Tapping into your artistic side inspires you to map new goals, and go after your dreams. It leads to a radiant chapter that inspires change. Overall, you can enjoy a new flow of energy, which gives you the green light to expand your horizons. You are a bright star, someone who has a gift to share with others. Making your mark on the world will bring about profound changes, it deepens the abundance possible in your life, this expansion captures the essence of freedom and imagination. Tremendous opportunities arrive to support a phase of growth, you have the dedication and motivation to achieve a top outcome.

SEPTEMBER WEEK FOUR

An inward journey is occurring for you soon. You are going through some changes, a shift leads to an evolution of your gifts. New talents are set to be revealed, it takes you on a journey where you can explore options, it widens your life in ways which connect you with other like-minded people. It is the beginning of a larger cycle which is likely to unfold over the next phase. An active aspect of advancement is coming. It is a time of growth on all levels. New information sweeps in to provide you with beautiful ideas and inspiration. You begin to see a larger picture of where you are headed, and what may be possible for you over the coming months. It's clearly a time of vision and planning. This provides you with reliable options you can bank on. You have highly creative talents, and they are going to hold you in good stead over the coming months. It does bring new options where you can grow your life in ways which give back to others, and this in itself is highly rewarding and beneficial to your life. You are a wonderful person who may, unfortunately, undervalue your own sense of self.

Additionally, the Equinox this week arrives to allow you the ability to harness the power of manifestation. Opportunities are coming into your life, which presents you with a compelling path forward. This sees a bond deepen with wildly supportive one, this person plays an essential role in the chapter ahead. It is a time which enables you to release bottled up emotions, it does bring strength into your life, and supports a bold section of growing a deeper bond. The extraordinary devotion and care this person display have you thinking big about future potential. There is advancement looming, which brings your situation to a new stage.

OCTOBER ASTROLOGY

October 1 - Full Moon in Aries.

The October full Moon is on the opposite side of the Earth as the Sun, and its face will be fully illuminated. This phase occurs at 21:05 UTC. This full moon is known as the Hunters Moon because at this time of year the leaves are falling, and the game is ready. This full moon is also known as the Travel Moon and the Blood Moon. This moon is also known as the Harvest Moon. The Harvest Moon is the full moon that occurs closest to the September equinox each year.

October 1 - Mercury at Greatest Eastern Elongation.

The planet Mercury reaches greatest eastern elongation of 25.8 degrees from the Sun.

October 7 - Draconids Meteor Shower.

The Draconids meteor shower runs annually from October 6-10 and peaks this year on the night of the 7th.

October 10 – Last Quarter Moon in Cancer.

This Moon phase occurs at 0.39 UTC.

October 13 – Mercury Retrograde begins in Scorpio.

During a retrograde period, it isn't the right time to move forward in any practical venture. Be prepared for misunderstandings and miscommunications to be more prevalent.

October 16 - New Moon in Libra.

The Moon will be on the same side of the Earth as the Sun and will not be seen in the night sky. This moon phase occurs at 19:31 UTC. This is an excellent time of the month to view galaxies and stars because there is no moonlight visible.

October 21, 22 - Orionids Meteor Shower.

The Orionids meteor shower runs yearly from October 2 to November 7. Orionids meteor shower peaks this year on the night of October 21 and the morning of October 22.

October 23 – First Quarter Moon in Capricorn.

This Moon phase occurs at 13.23 UTC.

October 31 - Full Moon, Blue Moon in Taurus.

The October full Blue Moon is on the opposite side of the Earth as the Sun, and its face will be fully illuminated. This phase occurs at 14:49 UTC. This is the second full moon in the same month, it is referred to as a blue moon.

October 31 - Uranus at Opposition.

The planet Uranus will be at its nearest approach to Earth, and its face will be illuminated by the Sun.

OCTOBER HOROSCOPE

OCTOBER WEEK ONE

You are doing the right thing by staying open to new environments, expanding your horizons opens your life to a new realm of possibilities. You shut the door on a problematic chapter soon, and harnessing an abundant outlook, you set off on a new adventure. This attracts positive outcomes, it stirs up a new flow of enticing options to explore. The past has been an enormous learning ground, it has given you the wisdom of the ages. You are currently in a cycle which has you turning towards a more spiritual path. It does lead to a chapter where you harness positive energies, and you do cross the road of individuals who bring new information and learning into your life. This can lead to sweeping changes, the fire in your belly is ignited, a passion for life sets you off on a new adventure. As you reflect on your passage through life, you can get a better understanding of how past events have shaped the person you are today. Your spirit is guiding you to advance your situation, paying attention to the subtle nuances of your thought processes does help pave the road ahead intuitively. It underscores the energy of magic, which is ready to emerge in your life and draw abundance into your world. You can reach for something more in your life, your spirit is guiding this progress, paying attention to your higher goals paves a road towards freedom and expansion. This liberates your potential, it takes you to a chapter which resonates warmly with the person you are becoming. Some fundamental changes are arriving which shift your focus forward, casting your net wide is a beautiful way to draw abundance.

OCTOBER WEEK TWO

The wheels are in motion, you are ready to embark on a chapter which makes the most of your talents. Your expertise is in a cycle of growth, it does bring in new areas, and it also helps you refine your gifts, and make the most of your abilities. You benefit from favorable events on the horizon, which lead towards a goal orientated chapter. A compelling path will open for you soon. This enables you to channel your talents in an area which resonates warmly with you. It does create a curious sideline for your excess energy and helps you develop a situation which is in alignment with your higher aspirations. This avenue is highly charged with positive options, it lets you plot a course towards achieving a substantial goal. There is a sign coming which enables you to spot an alternative which is practical, realistic, and rewarding. This avenue helps bridge the gap between your aspirations and tangible results. It's essential to create space for your own passions and dreams. You soon make your mark on the vision which holds promise. You have beautiful abilities and can quickly create space for something new in your life. Investigating options will give you the right boost to head towards a chapter which harnesses the power of your creativity. You are ready for advancement and would benefit from drawing abundance into your life. Plotting a course towards the right passion project will provide you with results. You are prepared to expand your horizons and seek new options. It gives you a much-appreciated boost, you are set to benefit from events on the horizon, which lead to a richly creative and expressive chapter. Harnessing your excess energy takes you to an area which is loaded with benefits. It is a time where you can rejoice and appreciate how far you have come on your personal journey.

OCTOBER WEEK THREE

You are in a time of reflection and healing. Doing this inner work does help you transition towards a new chapter. As you draw healing into your spirit, you harness the power within your tenacious core, resilience is a powerful tool which gives you strength. It's essential to think about decoding the puzzle of where to head; next, this will provide you with powerful inspiration. It does lead to a happier chapter. There will be a refreshing change for you soon, a stable and calming influence is coming into your life, this results in the sense of abundance and tranquility, which rejuvenates and renews your spirit. You create space to explore options and can contemplate the path ahead. It gives you a grounded foundation from which to grow your aspirations.

Additionally, outworn energy can be released, this makes room for something refreshing to follow. An inspiring phase coming for you, it brings a strong sense of balance into your life, you thrive in a stress-free environment, this holds you in good stead, you to take advantage of new opportunities which inspire and tantalize with exciting potential. It does provide you with fantastic growth, which feels empowering, you are ready to unleash your talents in a new area. Positive change is coming, it is a pivotal time where you can enter a bountiful cycle. As you move forward towards advancing your dreams, you are inspired by the changes ahead, which lead to adventure and excitement. This gateway towards a new life is something special, you feel a sense of buoyancy by the abundant and rewarding energy flowing into your life soon. Your perseverance to improve your situation and provide you with a phase of growth. In fact, refining your goals helps you spotlight an avenue which offers fruitful results.

OCTOBER WEEK FOUR

The rare Full Blue Moon this week says it is a time of abundance and magic. You face a crossroads which is all about contemplating the path ahead, choose wisely and by your higher vision as patterns which have limited progress in the past no longer restrict your way. A theme of abundance does guide a shift towards making headway on your long-term goals. This touches you down on a new area which inspires a great deal of growth for you. A breakthrough is coming, which enables you to turn a prominent corner and had towards growth. There is a steady burn of new potential simmering in your life. It does rekindle your motivation and enables you to plot a course towards achieving those larger goals. This chapter is a dynamic, changing, and evolving. It sees you shine in a new role soon, which is an impressive achievement and gives you the feedback needed to continue developing your goals. You face some tough decisions, you may be questioning the path ahead, and taking time to understand where your heart is leading does help you to solve the emotional strain you are currently under. It sets the stage for a chapter of growth to soon follow. Once restrictive or limiting areas are released, you enter a phase of rejuvenation. You are undergoing a time of growth and self-development, this guides you towards a situation which is vibrant and exciting. Sweeping changes arrive to herald a fresh start. This sees abundance flow into your world, as there is an emphasis on achieving a personal goal. Taking steps to follow where your intuition guides you do offer you a fantastic opportunity to transform your life. You begin to see more structure in your life, implementing a bold approach does create change while still keeping your sense of security stable and grounded.

NOVEMBER ASTROLOGY

November 3 - Mercury Retrograde ends in Libra.

You can now move forward with any delayed plans that you have been putting off due to the Mercury Retrograde phase. Relationships should soon improve as miscommunications resolve.

November 4, 5 - Taurids Meteor Shower.

The Taurids meteor shower runs yearly from September 7 to December 10. It peaks this year on the night of November 4.

November 8 – Last Quarter Moon in Leo.

This Moon phase occurs at 13.46 UTC.

November 15 - New Moon in Scorpio.

The Moon is on the same side of the Earth as the Sun and will not be visible in the night sky. This phase occurs at 5:07 UTC. This is an excellent time to view galaxies and star clusters because there is no moonlight visible.

November 17, 18 - Leonids Meteor Shower.

The Leonids meteor shower runs yearly from November 6-30. The Leonids meteor shower peaks this year on the night of the 17th and morning of the 18th.

November 22 – First Quarter Moon in Pisces.

This Moon phase occurs at 4.45 UTC.

November 30 - Full Moon in Gemini.

The November full Moon is on the opposite side of the Earth as the Sun, and its face will be fully illuminated. This phase occurs at 9:30 UTC. This full moon is known as Full Beaver Moon as this was the time of year to set beaver traps before the swamps and rivers froze. It is also known as the Frosty Moon and the Hunter's Moon.

November 30 - Penumbral Lunar Eclipse

A penumbral lunar eclipse occurs when the Moon passes through the Earth's partial shadow or penumbra. During this type of eclipse, the Moon will darken but not completely eclipse. This Penumbral lunar eclipse will be visible throughout most of North America, the Pacific Ocean, and northeastern Asia.

NOVEMBER HOROSCOPE

NOVEMBER WEEK ONE

The Taurids meteor shower which peaks on November 4th illuminates recent information regarding an influence surrounding your life, which could be holding back progress. However, exciting developments ahead enable you to reach a successful outcome on a goal you have been developing recently. It does bring foundations which have you feeling grounded, restored, and secure. This enables you to set your sights on a high area which builds on your dreams further. It sets in motion a path of inspiration which puts you in touch with a brilliant area to explore. This is nourishment for your mind and soul. You have an incredible ability to nurture others. You have been impacted by past events which have left an imprint on your soul. Forgiveness is a strong theme which emerges that will help you make peace with what has happened in your life. Creating space for healing will help nurture a more abundant environment, it leads to a chapter which is wiser, more settled, and definitely happier. Life picks up momentum as the news arrives, which heralds change. It does keep you on your toes, you enter a time where fast-moving information inspires change. The air of expectation is around you, this area is ready to blossom, it gives you a space you can sink your excess energy into. It is a path which is right for expansion and does guide you towards the attainment of knowledge and experience. A surprise is around the corner, as you open this news, your instincts fire up with sparks of inspiration. You feel this is an area which is bold and offers room for growth.

NOVEMBER WEEK TWO

You have an excellent ability to turn painful situations around and get the best out of whatever comes your way. Your imagination guides this process, you have a strong intuitive ability which heightens your personal awareness, it allows you to take advantage of your natural gifts, and this gives you a strong core of resilience. Fortune and luck are arriving soon to draw blessings into your world. There is much to look forward to, improvement is coming, it marks the start of a fresh chapter which ushers in an opportunity which supports your vision for future growth. This leads to exciting developments, you spread your wings and make a bold move towards progressing a substantial goal. Your creative input is valuable in this process as it makes the most of manifesting the best out of this area. You are ready to make strides towards a new area, it does help you reach a turning point. Taking a path which is expansive, bold, and creative, does expand your horizons and bring you to an exciting phase. Your mind thrives on new challenges, and projects. Your spirit welcomes opportunities which support growth and sees you forge new friendships.

NOVEMBER WEEK THREE

There are more extensive changes around your environment over the next phase. An opportunity crops up, which feels like the right fit, it becomes a bit of a passion project for you. At first, it's challenging to get this venture off the ground, and you come up with a remarkable solution which does see forward motion soon follow. It enables you to embrace a chapter where you achieve your goals. Exciting changes unfurl in your world soon. It does see you inviting dynamic and vibrant potential, which helps you initiate a path towards attaining a bountiful vision. As you seek out new opportunities, you reveal a route which offers growth and learning, crafting your idea, you embark on a journey towards the development of your dreams. It does signify a new beginning opens a gateway towards a happy chapter. It does lead to a branch of abundance and magic. Expanding your horizons enables you to enter a phase of robust growth. This person brings pleasant change into your life, it leads to a willingness to open your heart fully and take a leap of faith with someone who feels like a kindred spirit. It does bring harmony and joy, sharing thoughts and ideas in open communication feels like a breath of fresh air. You enter a new cycle where you develop a substantial goal over the coming months. It does provide you with a phase of growth, and this brings improvement into your life. As you begin to see the upgrades available for your hard work, you plant a seed which germinates into a blossoming phase of activity. It's a time which favors expansion, setting your imagination free is pivotal to unleashing these critical changes of essential growth.

NOVEMBER WEEK FOUR

This week you find progress is made with a pushy person, setting boundaries with this person provides you with a workable solution. The changes ahead clearly signify an expansion of goals for you. There are exciting developments ready to be revealed, this clears the decks, it enables you to embrace a new flow of potential into your surroundings. It does have you reaching for a substantial goal, and this sees a blur of hectic activity arrives, which leads to a highly productive chapter. You have an unusual ability to overcome challenges and head towards advancement. Setbacks are merely an invitation to persevere. This has held you in good stead over the years, and your ability to find solutions will also help you with future goals. An unexpected breakthrough provides you with a gateway to a new area. This is an exciting path which can be built upon. It is an unsettling time, yet one, which is ripe for expansion. Unexpected changes bring opportunities which allow you to break free of limitations. There is new potential simmering in the background, things will unfold and be fully revealed in time. Maintaining an optimistic and positive outlook is the best approach, this aids in manifesting the actual potential at the right time. You make significant headway on expanding your options soon. It takes you towards a life-changing phase, it is a path of evolution, and this gives you rock-solid foundations from which to grow your talents further. A greater sense of purpose holds you in good stead as you direct focused energy towards learning the field, which offers room for growth. An offer arrives soon after, and this reveals an exciting option.

DECEMBER ASTROLOGY

December 8 – Last Quarter Moon in Virgo.

This Moon phase occurs at 0.37 UTC.

December 13, 14,15 - Geminids Meteor Shower.

The Geminids meteor shower runs each year from December 7-17. The Geminids meteor showers peaks this year on the night of the 13th, 14th, and 15th. The nearly new moon this year will provide dark skies for an excellent show. Best viewing will be from a dim vista after midnight. Meteors will radiate from the constellation Gemini but can appear anywhere in the sky.

December 14 - New Moon in Sagittarius.

The Moon is on the same side of the Earth as the Sun and will not be visible in the night sky. This moon phase occurs at 16:17 UTC. This is an excellent time to view galaxies and stars because there is no moonlight visible.

December 21 – First Quarter Moon in Pisces.

This Moon phase occurs at 23.41 UTC.

December 21 - December Solstice.

The 2020 December solstice occurs at 10:02 UTC. The South Pole of the earth tilts toward the Sun, which, having reached its most southern place in the sky, is directly over the Tropic of Capricorn at 23.44 degrees south latitude. This December solstice also marks the first day of winter (winter solstice) in the Northern Hemisphere.

December 21 – Great Conjunction of Jupiter and Saturn.

A conjunction of Jupiter and Saturn will take place on December 21. This is known as the great conjunction as it is a rare celestial event. The last great conjunction occurred in the year 2000. The two bright planets will appear only 7 arc minutes of each other in the night sky. They will be so close that they will seem to make a bright double planet. Look to the west just after sunset for this impressive and rare planetary pair.

December 21, 22 - Ursids Meteor Shower.

The Ursids meteor shower occurs each year from December 17 - 25. This meteor event peaks this year on the night of the 21st and morning of the 22nd.

December 30 - Full Moon in Cancer.

The Moon is on the opposite side of the Earth as the Sun, and its face will be fully illuminated. This moon phase occurs at 03:28 UTC. This full moon is known as the Full Cold Moon because this is the time of year when the cold winters air arrives and nights become long and dark. This full moon is known as the Long Nights Moon and the Moon Before Yule.

DECEMBER HOROSCOPE

DECEMBER WEEK ONE

You may be feeling overwhelmed or drained because you been working too hard. If things have been busier than usual, it suggests that there are too much static and background noise occurring in your life. Slow down, limit commitments for a little while, and focus on restoring the harmony and getting things back to a more manageable state. This will invite abundance into your surroundings. You may feel as though you are facing a roadblock, you been working hard to achieve your goals, yet success seems temptingly just out of reach. It makes it difficult to see the road ahead, more information is arriving, which will help you progress a goal you have been hoping to achieve. It is a favorable time which enables you to head towards growth and open a new book of chapters. Goals on the home front are likely to reach fruition soon. Life is about to become busy, even hectic. You discover an option takes shape, and this becomes a more significant focus for you. Do your research, it is an area which requires due diligence to advance towards the highest outcome. Success is imminent, there is a proportion between the efforts expended and the rewards obtained. Streamline your situation so you can focus on achieving this goal. An opportunity to travel is on the cards, it helps you dial in the potential on a position which has been a compelling area of interest for you. You are concerned about what is going on in your life, but as you touchdown on a new chapter, you begin to feel more stable in this new landscape.

DECEMBER WEEK TWO

This week aligns you towards developing your situation, it takes you to a positive path that allows a breakthrough to be made. Your case is complicated, yet advancement is in motion. This takes you towards a chapter which offers transformation, as it unleashes your talents to stunning effect. You move towards a path which provides a new section of potential. Your vision guides this growth, and an offer arrives to support a phase which instigates sweeping changes. It is a time which feels dynamic and gives you the green light to expand your options. It may lead off the beaten track, but this puts you in contact with other curious individuals who offer fresh perspectives and lively ideas. It leads to a winning chapter, where you can embrace enthusiasm and expansion. It is an ideal time for setting intentions and directing your sense of purpose towards an ambitious goal. Exploring your options will provide you with excellent opportunities for growth. This fuels your motivation as you discover exciting avenues. Your inspiration is on the rise, it creates a climate which draws abundance into your world. You are ready to expand your horizons, it does bring you towards a beneficial chapter which opens a variety of new options. It takes you towards activities where you connect with diverse characters. This fuels the pool of potential, with many minds added to the mix, you discover some fantastic ideas to explore. Making a decisive move forward, you head in a direction which speaks to your heart.

DECEMBER WEEK THREE

There is a lot to be revealed soon regarding potential. You discover a situation blossoms with love and harmony. It helps you get back on course with your personal goals. You find out that you can take this connection to a deep and permanent place, it allows you to explore synergies with one who offers you a great deal of support. This brings new potential into your world and leads to a happier chapter. The sun shines in your social life soon with a magnetic connection forming with an innovative and enticing individual. This is someone you can share openly with, you communicate well with this kindred spirit. Connecting with this person does see your social life prosper, the magic emerges in your life. It leads to a time of bonding, as intimate thoughts are shared. It shines a light on security and new goals being possible. If things have felt quiet on the social front, you can expect a new flow of energy to sweep into this area to help shift things forward. It does lead to an expressive chapter that could bring a boon into your life. This begins a time of breakthroughs, it does allow more open and authentic communication to flow into your world. Knowing where you are headed with your personal life, creates the security you have been hoping for. A new beginning is marked for you. Releasing outworn energy does open the door to a brighter future. It is an important crossroads, focusing on abundance does help ease the disquiet which has been around your life. It signifies powerful healing is possible, you improve your situation, providing you with tangible results.

DECEMBER WEEK FOUR

This is a reflective cycle which gets you in touch with your higher goals, you can filter out distractions and plan your next chapter. Streamlining does enable you to focus on improving your circumstances. You are ready to embrace a chapter which draws more harmony into your surroundings, there is a shift occurring which offers you a robust area to develop. This kicks off a grand plan, which does connect with a substantial goal. You are ready to revolutionize and expand your life. This shift happens at this time of year, you have an acute sense of wanting to break free of limitations. This is guiding you towards expansion and discovery. Being in touch with your higher goals does broaden the scope of potential in your situation. Spend time setting goals, you are set to achieve a momentous outcome. You gain a broader understanding of where there have been issues in your mind recently. There is a great deal happening in your world, and it is helpful to take time out just for yourself, to restock and replenish your spirit. Releasing anxiety and doubt shifts you towards a direction of excitement and joy. You are leading up to a time which enables you to initiate an endeavor which holds promise. As you embark on a new chapter of potential, a project arrives, which draws your inspiration. This leads to building an area which inspires and reinvigorates your spirit. It is a creative time which enables you to shine. As you kick off towards achieving your grand plans, you draw a sense of abundance into your surroundings. It marks a new beginning and brings you joy. This is a fair indication that you are going to have more stability on the home front. It has been quite a journey for you this year, you can now set your sights on next years goals. It's a time to restore balance. You can clear the decks and prepare for a fresh chapter.

Dear Stargazer,

I hope you have enjoyed planning your year with the stars utilizing Astrology and Zodiac influences. My zodiac star sign books are released each year which detail a monthly list of astrological events, and a weekly (four weeks to a month) horoscope. You can find me on my Facebook page where you get loads of Astrology advice and information.

https://www.SiaSands.com

Feedback is welcomed and appreciated.

Many Blessings,

Sia Sands

www.ingramcontent.com/pod-product-compliance
Lightning Source LLC
Chambersburg PA
CBHW020334290526
45785CB00005B/2011